Real Estate Investing:

*A Newbie's Roadmap to Real
Estate Investing*

Daisy Christian

Table of Contents

Introduction

Congratulations on downloading this book and thank you for doing so.

The economy has made it hard to find full-time employment or to be paid enough money per hour to make ends meet. At the same time, things are now costing more and more money. People feel squeezed, and many of them have decided that they must find a way to create their own income.

Real estate has long been one answer for many people to climb out of a bad financial situation. In fact, many wealthy people made their fortunes in real estate. Some people become agents, and some of them go on to be brokers. Other people invest in properties.

You likely just need some basics of real estate, such as what kinds of real estate investing exist. You may wonder what your investment options are if you have very little money saved up to invest in property. Finally, nobody wants to get into legal trouble during the process of making a financial turnaround. Well, you have purchased the right book.

The following chapters will discuss four different options for real estate investing. Two of them can be done by people who have very little money going into it. Of course, all four options are doable by people who have some money saved or the ability to borrow a large amount of money.

There are plenty of books on this subject on the market. Thank you again for choosing this one! Every effort was made to ensure it is full of as much useful information as possible, please enjoy!

Chapter 1: Get the Mindset

The economy makes it hard for many people to make ends meet. Some of us get into real estate investing to gain control over our financial future. Some of us even dream of becoming wealthy in real estate. That is because we know that it is one of the fastest ways to become wealthy. Since you are reading this book, you are obviously considering getting into the real estate racket.

Preparatory Mental Exercises

The wealthiest real estate investor in the country, Cody Sperber, got there by having a mentor who pushed him beyond his comfort zone. The mentor also had the young entrepreneur do a few exercises to prepare his mind for success in real estate investing. Here is what the mentor had him do:

1) Ask yourself why you want to do real estate. Beyond just the money, what are your other motivations to obtain financial security or even wealth? Do you want to travel? Do you want to help out your mother? Do you have debts you need to pay off to rebuild your credit? For many people, the money part is a vehicle to something else that is the real reason they want the money.

2) Create a vision board. This is a poster board where **you create a collage** that includes magazine pictures, words, etc., that help you visualize your ultimate goal. It motivates you during the times you will need motivation.

3) Write down daily affirmations. Write down what you are grateful for and what your goals are. Read them at least once daily. This will help you to focus and change your mindset. It will even start to change your surroundings.

4) Write your eulogy. You read that right. This one will get your attention when you go to write it as well because it will make you think about what other people would have to say about you at this moment in time. After you obtain your financial goals, you will have done things for other people that will make their opinions and memories of you change.

5) Realize that there is nothing that you can't get through to obtain your goals. Winning is a combination of venturing out into the unknown, having the right mindset, determination, and having the right tools.

Assess Your Skills

Everyone is good at some things and bad at other things. The successful real estate investor does not avoid the things they don't do well. They deal with them. Attack what you lack! If you don't take care of these things, they will create bigger problems for you down the road.

For instance, if you have the gift of gab, but you are disorganized in the office, take a month or so and handle the office stuff. Deal with it and get a routine down. Then hire somebody to do the routine you established as soon as you can afford to hire somebody. In the meantime, don't neglect those things you are not good at or hate to do.

Prepare Yourself for Some Self-Discipline

When poor people receive a large sum of money, from a lump sum retirement payout, inheritance money from the death of a loved one, etc, they squander it. They buy showy items like a new car or they take friends out to eat, etc. What could have paved the way to a bright future is wasted in no time flat.

To be a successful real estate investor, you need to reinvest a portion of the money that you make into marketing. You need to become a master at marketing too. Prepare yourself to wait a while before buying the big-ticket items that you really want to buy.

When you finally have the new car, house, other things you want, you will feel pride that you earned them, and not guilty that you squandered money to get them. They represent just a percentage of what you actually earned. While that is not as showy as you might be tempted to be, you will have the peace of mind that comes with knowing you have built yourself a money-making machine and that poverty will not return to your world.

Get the Millionaire Mindset

Cody, that young millionaire real estate investor, had some tips for changing one's mindset to think like a millionaire.

1) Wealthy people think differently than most people do. Wealthy people are positive, confident souls. The key thing is that they face fear. They don't back away from things they have no experience with or are not good at.

2) Wealthy people take purposeful action. The millionaires that earned their money, rather than inheriting or winning it, took action. They did what it took to make that money.

3) Wealthy people are not afraid of making mistakes. You will make some financial, social, time-wasting, and/or other mistakes. The key is to learn from the mistakes and continue to get better at your craft.

4) Wealthy people realize that accountability is everything. Focus on what you are doing and have somebody else hold you accountable for what you do.

5) Wealthy people believe that they deserve to be successful. Lots of people squander financial opportunities that come their way that could change their future because deep-down, they feel that they don't deserve to have financial success. If you feel that way, change your thinking.

6) Wealthy people are committed and focused. They commit to the goals they set for themselves, and focus on attaining those goals.

7) Wealthy people surround themselves with winners. Whether your realized it or not, the people you hang around influence your thinking and your habits. When you change your friends to winners, their ways will "rub off on" you.

Chapter 2: Four Strategies Overview

There are four types of real estate investments that are discussed in this book. Some take more mental work while others take more physical work (or the hiring of it done). Some take upfront cash while others do not. Some are short-term while others are long-term investments.

If you don't have much money, that will limit the investment options you have going into it, but you can work up to the other options as you go. Do you want to make long-term investments or quick cash? You will need to have that aspect figured out as well.

Maybe you're willing and able to start different types of real estate investing. If you have money right now to invest, the sky is the limit because you can maximize many different opportunities that come along.

SCENARIO 1) You have a little money, and you want quick cash.
INVESTMENT STRATEGY: *Quick flips ("wholesaling")* – In this strategy, you find a motivated seller and get them under a contract. You then sell the contract to a buyer/investor who wants to fix and flip (or make money some other way). You both make money because you got the property under contract at a very low price and successfully negotiated with both parties. You are not actually investing money, but time and effort to get some quick cash.

SCENARIO 2) You have a little money, and you want long-term wealth.

INVESTMENT STRATEGY: *Creative investments* – In this situation, you are able to do a rent-to-own deal but somebody else rents the place and pays you. You make your payments with their money. Eventually, you own the property.

SCENARIO 3) You have money to invest, access to other people's money, and you want quick cash from your investments.

INVESTMENT STRATEGY: *Fix and flips (rehabs)* – This is a common one where a house or some other type of property needs some work done on it to make it more appealing and valuable to a conventional buyer. You can fix it up yourself or you can hire it to be done. Maybe you just get the fixer upper at a steal and don't do any work on it. Whatever you do to it, you then sell it at a profit.

SCENARIO 4) You have money to invest, or access to other people's money, and want long-term wealth from your investments.

INVESTMENT STRATEGY: *Buy and hold* – In this strategy, you buy property that you eventually pay off. You rent it out and all of that money, minus maintenance and taxes, is pure profit. Maybe you live in it for a while. Either way, the value of property typically increases with the time. You can unload it after several years, and during a peak time in the housing market to get a huge payday.

Chapter 3: Quick Flips

"Quick flips" is another word for wholesaling. This is the strategy that a person can use if they have little money to work with and they want to make quick money. This strategy has become popular because it does not require a person to buy property up front. Therefore, it is seen as the way for a person with no money to work up to becoming a fix and flipper or a landlord.

The basic way that this works is that you find people who are motivated to sell their home or other property...so motivated to sell their property they will let it go for very little money.

Then you get them to sign an "assignable contract," which means that you can reassign the contract to somebody else. You have every intention of reassigning the properties because you are the middle man/woman who matches sellers with buyers who are themselves investors who want to profit from the property.

The property must, therefore, be obtained cheaply enough to make both you and the investor/buyer a profit, accounting for the money it will take the investor/buyer to repair and rehabilitate the property.

You need to be (or willing to become) the type of person who does a lot of dealing with people one on one. You also have to view what you are doing as a service for people who need to get out of a bad situation rather than thinking of this as a way to take advantage of people. The prospects have the option to try to sell their properties themselves or to spend the extra time and a chunk of the sales price by using realtors.

Chapter 7 shows many different ways you can find motivated sellers. They include putting out bandit signs, using social media, approaching people who break the codes for the height of their grass, people who are getting evicted, burned-out landlords, Craigslist, "bird dogs" (scouts), postcards, expired real estate listings, dispersing advertising pens, knocking on doors, or sending automated emailers whenever someone provides their contact information on your website.

To break this down even further here is what you do:

1. **Get yourself organized.**

   The ledger - It is advisable to make a spreadsheet to keep all of the basic information about all of your prospects. Somebody who won't budge on their price today may change their mind tomorrow. You would do well to have everything about that person and their property right at your fingertips.

   Real estate agents do this as well. Some even print off a copy each night to be ready for phone calls during the evenings.

   The phone system - If you are on an extremely tight budget, you could just set up a Google Voice phone number to handle your incoming calls so that your personal phone won't be ringing constantly. Or you could go ahead and give your phone number out and answer all calls as they come in.

The organizational system - If you can afford to do it, get yourself a computerized system that handles all aspects of your business. This system is generally called a customer relations manager, or "CRM" for short. It is the system that sends automated emails and other follow-up things over a period of several days to the prospects to warm them up and keep your name in front of them. It also computes figures that you enter and analyzes deals. Real Estate Mogul could get you hooked up with one of these and a mentor.

Of course, you can keep track of various prospects cheaply by doing everything manually, perhaps organizing yourself with what is called a "come-up" file where file cards are filed by date in a file cabinet drawer or something similar. These have been utilized by underwriters and other businesses over the years.

You write down on the card what action you last took with a prospect and what the prospect said or did. You write on the card what you need to do next with that prospect and on what day you need to do it. Then you file the card under that date.

When that day comes around, you take that card out of the file cabinet, get the corresponding physical file and do whatever you need to do...send an email, call them, etc. Notate what you did and write the next date and activity you plan to do concerning the prospect on the card.

File the card under that date you wrote. File the physical file where it belongs for easy access the next time you need it. You could also just have everything about the various accounts in Word on your computer.

A simple pocket organizer may also do the trick when you are just starting out and are on a tight budget.

2. **Figure out/set up how you want to find your leads.**

Investigate. Go knock on doors and ask questions. When you see "For Rent" signs in lawns, that have high grass, write down the address and phone number. Go to the courthouse and find out the names and numbers of code breakers who likely can't afford the fine. Form an agreement with a real estate agent who lets you see the expired MLS listings. If you witness an eviction, as is evident by a move going on while at least one sheriff is present, and approach those people to inquire about their situation. You research online.

People will likely want a business card, either because they are serious about keeping in touch with your or because it is an easy way to get rid of you. If you can afford them, it looks professional.

Online advertising - Advertising on Craigslist under the "Etc" category is free, but the site is also swamped with people doing what you are doing. You could also use social media.

Bird dogs - You could also use bird dogs (scouts) who get paid out of the proceeds at the time of the closing on any properties they find.

Bandit signs - As soon as you can afford to have them made, you need to get yourself some bandit signs to advertise your contact information and the fact that you are buying properties for fast cash. You can use many other of the listed lead generation methods.

Postcards – Mail out about 2,500 cards, and you may get a return of about three deals. While it may cost you $1,250 to mail that many post cards, just three small deals that together net you $5,000 would quadruple your money.

A website - If you can afford to invest more money, get a website and include the website on your bandit signs.

Include a "squeeze page" on your website that gets the visitor to give you their contact information on an online form. Set the system up to also email you whenever somebody fills out one of the online forms.

Ideally, you will want to set up a website for different markets and also for buyers and for sellers in each market. That will take some money and/or time to set up.

3. **Contact and get to know the prospect.**

You found your leads in person, online, or they left you a voicemail message. Whatever the method, there will come a time when you talk to a prospect for the first time.

Have a basic script that you memorize to answer typical questions. Other than answering their questions with as little detail as possible, you have four goals for this initial contact. You want to:

1. Build rapport with them. Spend time building a relationship. Know what you can about them, figuring out *who* they are.
2. Find out *why* they want to sell their property. Beyond wanting money, what is it that they really need?
3. Find out their *bottom price* they would take for their property.
4. Set up an *appointment* for another phone call. Don't skip this because you need to develop a relationship with that person to get them to know, like, and trust you. People they know, like and trust will be the only ones who have a chance to make a deal with them.

Of course, if you are talking to the them in person, you will also have to try to get their *contact information.* If you discover that their price is too high, then they are not motivated enough. If they don't want to talk to you again, they are not motivated enough. Since what you do only works when you have motivated sellers who will let their properties go at low prices, write these people off. You don't want to waste any more time on them.

4. **Analyze the situation.**

At this stage, you consider "comps,". This is a market comparison to see what it would be worth if fixed up, how much it would cost to fix it up, how much profit a buyer would need, how much profit you would need, etc. Then you (or the CRM) crunch the numbers to find out whether or not the seller's price is low enough to accept.

5. **Meet the seller and make your offer.**

You've done the analysis and you know how much money you can offer the seller. If the seller is local, meet them at the property with an assignable contract form in hand and make the offer there. If they are not local, make the offer over the phone and send the assignable contract to them to sign online.

If they sign the contract, open an escrow so a third party will hold the earnest money until both parties meet their obligations as stated in the contract. Keep things moving forward.

6. **Negotiate with sellers who won't lower sales price.**

If the seller won't accept your offer because they want to hold out for a bigger amount of money, tell the prospect that you'll have to run their price by your "higher authority" person (maybe your wife) and then come back and say that the authority person said the seller's price was too high. This is a non-aggressive way to negotiate with the seller to get the price down.

If that didn't work, you could come back later and take a slightly harder line with the seller and tell them the buyer set a seven-day deadline to take your (low-ball) offer or the seller will lose their chance to quickly unload the property.

If you can't get the price lowered, but you have the finances to do other types of investing, you can explore those other options if the deal is not good enough for wholesaling.

For instance, maybe you decide to buy the property instead of selling the contract. Fix up the property and sell it or rent it out.

7. **Sell the deal.**

There are several negotiation strategies you can use on the buyer side of the equation. You can 1) send the offer to buyers, 2) syndicate the offer online, 3) post it in the classifieds, or 4) co-wholesale the offer with other investors.

Caution

A few words of caution are necessary if you are considering using the quick flipping/wholesaling strategy.

Wholesaling appears to be illegal in some states, but legal in other states. The heart of the matter is that wholesaling involves duties that are similar to a real estate agent, but no license is acquired.

Real estate agents take the time, trouble, and expense to learn their state's educational requirements and then to pass a national licensing exam. With no licensure required, wholesaling is not sanctioned by a board and has no oversight body.

Wholesalers argue that they merely locate properties, as a scout/bird dog would, and then facilitate meetings between buyers/investors and motivated sellers while using assignable contracts to take the contracts out of their hands and into those of the buyers/investors.

It seems to be somewhat hard to find out the legality of the practice from state to state online. Perhaps that is because quick flipping/wholesaling is just now becoming popular.

Since a real estate lawyer is required by some states to be present at the closing of real estate property, it would be likely that a real estate lawyer would know about the legality of wholesaling in your state or could easily find out about it.

If a real estate lawyer is required at closings in your state, a real estate lawyer would also cut a check to your bird dog if a bird dog provided the lead to you about the property being sold, which lends some credibility to wholesaling. If you like the lawyer that you ask, you may consider asking him if he would want to work with you in your future wholesaling endeavors.

Wholesalers often operate under a sole proprietorship or LLC and then have a group of people they normally do business with, such as a real estate lawyer, an inspector, and a group of buyer/investors they normally offer real estate bargains to first.

Although this is the case, another thing that may come back on a wholesaler is if the wholesaler presents himself to a prospective client in a manner that suggests he is part of a large company when in fact he just works for himself. A client might find this unnerving.

Additionally, while the assignable part of the contract is there, it is often not mentioned by wholesalers that reassigning the contract is an almost certainty because it might make their prospect uncomfortable with doing business with you.

While some people many not care about these kinds of, if and when they find out about them, other clients may feel they have been played for a fool and/or become concerned as to whether the whole deal was legally done. Make sure that it was!

Once you get those kinds of things out of the way, you will need to be aware of typical rookie mistakes that people new to this business make. They are as follows:

1. *Having no emergency cash* – The whole appeal of this strategy is the fact that it does not require a person to have a lot of money to get into the game. However, things like bandit signs and marketing can take more money than people usually assume.

   The bigger threat, however, is that you must find a way to actually purchase the property that you put under contract if you do not find a buyer for it!

2. *Having no list of buyers in advance* – Rookies often wait until they put a property under contract to start to locate buyers. This not only threatens to leave the rookie wholesaler having to purchase the property, but it leaves the wholesaler no bargaining power to make much profit on the deal when a buyer is finally found. The buyer will likely sense the rookie's level of desperation.

   It would be better to network at REIA meetings, notating names and what types of properties the buyers/investors normally prefer to purchase. Go ahead and form friendships with these people. That way, they'll know who you are when you present them with offers.

3. *Ignoring what the buyer needs* – Rookies need to realize that the buyer/investor needs to profit from the deal, just like you do. If the property you offer to them requires a whole lot of rehabilitation to be done on it,

rookies need to understand that the buyer needs to get the property cheap enough to profit after spending time and/or money for extensive rehabilitation.

Be willing to take less money if you are unloading a big project that you did not get under contract at a low enough price. Don't tick off your buyers or they may not deal with you. They may give you a bad reputation just as you are trying to establish yourself. Do them right.

4. *Failing to get property inspected* – Sellers will sometimes unload properties because the properties have significant problems, such as mold problems or gas leaks. Other sellers are not aware of problems that lurk.

   Whether or not the seller knows about problems with the properties, their problems become your problems if you, the wholesaler, do not get the properties inspected before putting them under contract because all properties will be inspected whenever you find prospective buyers.

   If you put properties under contract that nobody will buy because of significant lurking problems, you will be responsible for purchasing them, just as you would if you purchased the property to keep it for yourself.

   Wholesalers, therefore, need to have properties inspected before putting them under contract, no matter how good of a bargain they appear to be or what assurances you get from sellers.

5. *Paying too much* – The whole point to wholesaling is to buy properties cheap enough to allow profit for both the wholesaler and the buyer/investor. Wholesalers can't

expect buyers/investors to overprice their properties to make up for wholesalers not getting properties for them cheaply enough!

Yet, some newbie wholesalers can't walk away from bad deals or successfully renegotiate with sellers. Others just don't pay enough attention to the numbers they need to crunch before making offers.

6. *Not crunching the numbers* – If you get this right, much of the other stuff on this list will fall into place.

   Before making an offer, wholesalers must get a reliable "after repair value" (ARV) for the property from a real estate broker. Yes, you need to establish a relationship with one or more agents. Maybe you pay them a fee for every time you utilize their services. Offer something that they get in return.

   Figure what 70% of the ARV is. From that number, subtract your wholesaler's fee, which is usually a few thousand dollars.

   The number you come up with is the "maximum allowable offer" (MAO). To put the property under contract at a price higher than the MAO, puts your profit at risk.

7. *Buying a bad foreclosure* – The economic recession in the United States has created a lot of foreclosures. Some of them are offered for sale at well below the market value, but could have problems that an inspector needs to find. They are often trashed or sabotaged by their former owners who were forced from them. They could also have several liens against them.

If you can see them for yourself, have them inspected, etc., this would not be a huge problem. However, you are not allowed to have foreclosed properties inspected. You cannot even look inside of them yourself. That being the case, you could end up with expensive problems if you put these under contract...unsellable and possibly things that just continue to cost you money!

Be sure you have enough money to afford to take losses on these. If you ignore this advice, and depend on foreclosures to make your business, they could very well break your business.

Purchasing "real estate owned" (REO) properties is a better option. REOs are bank-owned properties that the bank bought from the home-owners. These homes have clear titles (other than the bank owners), and they are much less likely to have been trashed or sabotaged by their former owners. Like foreclosures, they are low in price, but you are allowed to have them inspected.

8. *Poor marketing* – You need to market both your properties and yourself or else you will struggle in this business. You need to have lots of options for buyers at your disposal instead of, out of desperation, bending to the will of the one buyer/investor that you finally find.

9. *Bad market pricing* – Don't set your prices too high or you won't find buyers. If you find you have set a price too high, email or snail mail letters to the same potential buyers that you are willing to negotiate your price down. This will lure at least one of them to you.

Chapter 4: Creative Investments

Creative investments are for investors who don't have much money, but have the goal of long-term wealth. The term, "creative investments" refers to any type of buying or selling that is non-traditional in nature.

People often think of unscrupulous practices when they hear the term, "creative investments," because of the pyramid schemes and confidence tricks of the 20th and the 21st centuries, but not all of them are underhanded.

Bird Dogging

Even though you would technically be trading your scouting services for money, this is a popular area for future investors to start their careers, especially if they have little to no money.

Similar to quick flippers/wholesalers, bird dogs locate properties that can be picked up cheaply by buyer/investors. However, bird dogs have no more to do with the process than to locate the properties, get the owners' contact information and other information, report it to wholesalers (who then snag a buyer), and collect a $500 referral fee from the wholesaler's attorney at the time of closing on the property.

Sometimes bird dogs arrange a partnership, a "joint venture agreement," if they are not legally allowed to collect referral fees because of not being a real estate agent, etc. Whatever the legal arrangement has to be, the bird dog just scouts for good deals and gets paid for their services whenever the wholesaler closes on properties the bird dog referred.

The Sandwich Lease Agreement

This is the lesser-known type of the two rent-to-own options, the other option being a straight forward Purchase Lease option. Realize that this is not a "subject-to" arrangement because you would technically be just a renter, not a new owner of the property until you pay it off in full.

A sandwich lease option would gives you the opportunity to buy the house (cheaply) within one to five years with the ability to sublet the property out to somebody else (at a profit) who is also interested in buying the house with rent-to-own financing.

In the Sandwich Lease option, you find a motivated seller of a house and negotiate a really low monthly payment. Try to avoid paying the nonrefundable option premium. Negotiate no future valuing, no rent credit, and as much as you can get in the details that would favor you. Make sure that the contract gives you the right of assignment (a "lease option" so that you can sublet the property).

After you get your low-priced deal made with the seller, you find a person who also wants a purchase lease option, luring them in with an attractive, somewhat low monthly payment (but still more money than you pay monthly).

The person you will likely sublet the property to may just want to try the house out before deciding to buy it. Maybe they are military people who have an unsure future. They may be a couple who can't qualify for traditional financing, etc.

Negotiate with them for better terms for yourself, such as an upfront option payment of two to three percent of the property's value, etc. You offer rent credit and you apply the down payment to the financed purchase price. Have a lender pre-qualify the prospective tenant based on what their situation will likely be in two years.

The tenant buyer will basically be paying you money that you use to pay your own rent-to-own house payments, and you make some extra money with each payment.

If your tenant buyer tells you they want to buy the property, then the tenant buyer, you, and the seller all three meet at the time of the closing and close all of the purchase lease arrangements, transferring the ownership from the seller you've been paying to your tenant buyer who has been paying you. The original owner got out of a bad financial situation, you made some money, and the new owner owns a home where he has resided at a fair price, and is happy with.

If your tenant does not buy the property at the end of their lease, you keep all of the money that you were paid. If you are at the end of your own lease agreement, you can pay off the remainder of what you owe and keep the property and do with it what you want to from then on. If you cannot or don't want to pay it off, you have the option to just walk away from it per the agreement you signed with the homeowner. You made money with your tenant while you had both the lessor and the lessee.

This arrangement works well when the housing market is bad and homes just aren't selling. There will be a lot of motivated sellers in a bad economy. Your profit potential would be between 20 and 30 percent of the home's value for every home that you make sandwich lease agreements on and put good tenants into!

You could also hedge your bets by having several of these contracts going. That way, you could take that 20 to 30 percent to pay for the costs incurred by the few problem tenants.

Caution

Several things could go wrong after you enter into this sort of investment. Problems could come from either the lessor side of the equation or from the lessee side of it.

Tenant falls behind on payments - One scenario that is quite possible is that your tenant could fall behind on making his payments to you, forcing you to make your payments to the homeowner from money that you have saved up or from some other source.

To default on your agreement with the seller will breach your rent-to-own contract, which you had signed as an investment opportunity. Don't let a tenant have the power to ruin your investment opportunity. While it technically doesn't take much money to get into this racket, it also doesn't take much of a cash shortage to end this dream for you.

Tenant neither pays rent nor leaves the property - A tenant could fail to pay you and also refuse to leave the property, forcing you to wait longer to finally get the person evicted. You'll have to sue them for unpaid rent and wait for that money. Other things like that could happen.

Be sure to screen a tenant before you sublet to him to have a better chance to avoid this situation from happening. If you don't have a lot of money saved up going into this arrangement, it will be very important that you screen potential tenants so that you will get a good one. Then save up the extra money for times down the road when you will need to make payments between renters or pay for costs that may come about from having bad or unlucky tenants.

A sandwich lease agreement tenant may be hard to find - The public could just as easily shop for the home of their dreams using a realtor's MLS and get it with a normal purchase lease agreement. You need to find somebody who likes your property in particular. Therefore, it may be hard to find a tenant who will go for the sandwich lease option. While you are looking for that tenant, you still need to make your monthly payments to the homeowner.

When the economy improves, there are fewer motivated sellers - The homeowner could negotiate a better deal for themselves, so you really need to find the motivated sellers. It would be easier to find highly motivated sellers during a bad economy.

Your seller could default on making their mortgage payments - While you are faithfully making your payments to the homeowner and hoping to own the property one day, the homeowner may be in such a bad financial situation that they are not making their mortgage payments. They could file bankruptcy or get sued. Desperate, motivated sellers could very easily be tempted to treat your money as rental income and ignore the purchasing option part of the agreement.

To have a record of intention, which the seller would not be legally able to deny, record your lease or indicate in a different manner that you intend to purchase the property. Something that appears on the title at the time that you make the sandwich lease agreement with the motivated seller may suffice.

You can cover yourself with an escrow account that a third party manages, which makes sure the seller's mortgage payments are paid while you are paying the seller your monthly payments.

The Cooperative Agreement

This technique is to be used with sellers who are not desperate and want to maintain control in the selling process. In this arrangement, you will use one contract. You will have a rent-to-own option with the seller, then you will find a tenant that the seller must also approve of. You collect a fee, which you could put toward the purchase price.

Short Sale or Pre-Foreclosure

A foreclosure process starts with the lender filing a public, and recorded, notice of default (after the mortgage has not been paid for several months). You or some other investor will offer to purchase the property for a price that is less than what is owed on the mortgage. The homeowner and the lender have to agree to the price. When the property is sold, the homeowner is responsible for all taxes for the mortgage payments not paid.

Land Trust to Acquire Foreclosed Properties

Land trusts have normally been used as non-profit entities to own property, but they have recently been used to obtain properties that are in foreclosure. This practice allows homeowners to keep their homes while also allowing investors to receive incredible returns on their investments.

Some people think that this type of trust does not cause due-on-sale clauses that would force the refinancing of the property, but that is only true when the borrower has been and continues to be a beneficiary of the trust and does not pertain to the transfer of the rights of occupancy in the property.

This type of trust makes it more difficult for a lender to know that a transfer has happened, but not impossible. If the lender discovers a transfer has taken place, the lender can accelerate the loan. However, legally, a transfer to a trustee in this sort of trust cannot be called a due-on-sale violation unless 100% of the beneficiary's interest is transferred to somebody else. Therefore, a beneficiary interest of up to 99% can be assigned to a co-beneficiary with no recourse from a lender, such as the due-on-sale penalty.

A "remainder agent" is used in traditional trusts. They are appointed to be responsible for the trust if the beneficiary dies or is incapable of performing the duties. A land trust, however, is a beneficiary directed trust instead of a trustee-directed trust. As such, a remainder agent could be a remainder beneficiary instead of a remainder trustee, as would be done if it were a normal trustee-directed trust.

Chapter 5: Fix and Flips

This option is one of the easiest of all of the options, and a lot of people do it. All you need is money or access to money (a loan) to buy a fixer-upper property and the stuff needed to rehab it or hire it rehabbed. Then you just sell it at a profit.

You could just buy it and turn around and sell it through a realtor without rehabbing it if the purchase price is low enough. This is an option if you are a quick flipper/wholesaler who couldn't quite get the seller to bring the price down low enough to give both you and a buyer/investor a profit.

If you hire contract work, you need to have a copy of the forms that contain the items listed on the last pages of this chapter.

You will have to do some form of marketing when you are ready to sell your masterpiece. Here are a few options that you have:

Stage - After the punch list (see below) items are completed and the contractors have left, stage the home as needed so that it would show well to prospective buyers.

Price – Check new comps. Figure out what your pricing strategy will be. Determine the buyer and selling agent incentives, such as warranty, bonus, closing costs, etc.

Signs – Put directional signs close to the corner. Put a sign in the property's yard. Place an informational box that is full of flyers in the yard.

MLS – Select a realtor. Take photos, write the listing description. List your property on the MLS.

Website – Put your property listing on your own website with the room sizes, directions, incentives and the nearby attractions.

Internet marketing – Post YouTube video clips of your property and links to your website on Craigslist every two days.

Promote video – Buy a fiverr.com gig to promote YouTube video.

Social media – Promote your property on Facebook, Linkdin, Twitter and on Pinterest.

Mobile marketing – Create QR codes for your website and YouTube video. Embed them into your property flyer.

Flyer – Create flyers. Place them into an informational box, and put the box in the yard of the property and in the kitchen.

Water – Put bottled water into the refrigerator. Put a note on the fridge to the buyer and the realtors that says the water is there for them to enjoy.

Caution

As is the case with all of the strategies, there are things you need to watch out for even when doing this easy strategy.

First of all, make sure the title is clear when you buy the property.

Secondly, make sure you are protected if you hire people to rehabilitate your property. Any kind of injury could happen that would tempt people to gain monetarily by suing you if you did not take precautionary steps.

You will need to make sure that the people you hired are licensed, insured, etc., and that you have been able to check off all of the other items on the "Contractor Job Flow" that is on the next page.

If you took all of the responsible measures before, during, and after work was done, you would prevent any such lawsuit from coming about.

Contractor Job Flow

Set-Up for New Contractor

1. *Contractor's license* - class A, B, C, trades (electrical, plumbing, HVAC)
   Class A: A single contract they work can be worth up to $120,000.
   Class B: A single contract they work can be worth up to $7,500.
   Class C: A single contract they work can be worth up to $1,000.

   Verify that they are licensed with the state board.

2. *Insurance* – injuries to others and general liability for property plus worker's comp for the death of or injured worker's if there are three or more employees

   Obtain a copy of the contractor's insurance certificate.

3. *W-9* – form for IRS 1099 reporting

Obtain a copy of the W-9 form.

Before the Work Begins

4. *Contractor indemnification agreement* – ratified agreement and indemnification

Obtain a completed agreement.

Job Close-Out

5. *Final inspection* plus the *punch list*

   Confirm these were completed.

6. *Final payment* and *close-out*

   Obtain a lien release waiver.

Indemnification Agreement

I, _____

[Contractor Name], agree to the following:

1. To the fullest extent of the law, the General Contractor or the Subcontractor, shall defend, indemnify and hold harmless [Your Name] (Contractor) from any and all claims for bodily injury and/or property damage that may arise from performance of the General contractor's or the Subcontractor's work to the extent that is caused by the negligence or the intentional acts of the General Contractor's or the Subcontractor's, General Contractor's or Subcontractor's subcontractors, or of anyone directly or indirectly employed by the General Contractor's Subcontractor.

_____

Signature

_____

Printed Name

_____

Business Title

_____

Today's Date

Punch List

Date:_____

Address:_____

Owner:_____

Contractor:_____

<u>Item Description</u>   <u>Location</u>   <u>Date Completed</u>

_____

_____

_____

_____

_____

_____

_____

_____

_____

Waiver of Lien

For the value received, the undersigned hereby waives ALL of his or her rights and claims for construction lien for the labor, material or the services performed on, or provided to, land and improvements located on the property located at
_____, _____, owned by
_____ regarding a
Project on which _____
acted as the Contractor.

Dated this _____ day of _____, 20_____

Contractor Name:

_____

Signature:

_____

Chapter 6: Buy and Hold

The cost of just about everything is going up. Real estate been a way for people obtain wealth for a long time. This is obvious by the fact that the average homeowner has a net worth of about $174,000 while renters have a net worth of around $5,100.

People who have the money to purchase property when they are young have a golden opportunity to increase wealth throughout their lives. A person can make money merely by buying homes in his younger years when the value of homes dip, holding onto the homes for many years, and then selling them toward the end of his life at a time when the price of homes is high.

A guy like that would likely live in one of the homes and rent out the other ones for decades while the homes also increase in value. This is the epitome of the common phrase, "It takes money to make money," and boy what money that man would make!

Most of us, however, spend our whole lives just paying for one house. Then we sell it at the end of our lives and use the money for healthcare or something else we need when we are old. If we have done fairly well, however, we can afford to hang onto it and give it to a child as an inheritance.

It is possible for people at any age to profit from buying and holding homes or other property. Many middle-aged people commonly have a few thousand dollars saved up or can get a loan. A person could find property at a bargain price, fix it up and hold onto it for a few years, getting rental income while holding it and then sell it when the price of homes increase and the person no longer wants to deal with rental homes or renters.

If a person has little money going into real estate investment, that person could start out doing one of the creative investment techniques or do wholesaling for a while, build up their savings, and then graduate to fix and flips or buy/fix and holds.

Whichever a person does and whenever a person starts, that person can likely make at least some decent amount of money from buying and holding property.

There are actually several reasons why buying and holding property makes a person money.

1. **Income**

    Not only do houses and other properties increase in value over time, but they can often be rented out for rental income during the years the investor owns them. Rental income is often enough to cover the payments on property. Once the property is paid for in full, the rental income becomes pure profit.

2. **Depreciation**

    After your property gets to be over 27 ½ years old, the IRS lets you start to write off part of the value of your property. That makes its value negative income, which significantly decreases the amount of tax that you owe, likely even wiping it out. Take the maintenance costs out of the rental income too.

3. **Equity Build-Up**

The rental income pays the mortgage payment. As you go along, part of the principle amount owed is paid down, giving you equity.

4. **Appreciation**

The property can go up or down in value. Sometimes, the market crashes as it did back in 2007. Long-term, however, real estate has increased in value an average of about 4.62% per year. Appreciation is the exponential growth of the investor's equity as the property is held longer.

5. **Leverage**

Both stocks and real estate go up in value over the long-term. You just need to be able to survive the downturns with a positive cash flow. Leveraging involves the use of somebody else's money to create positive cash flow.

For instance, a person could take $20,000 and gamble with it in the stock market. If they are lucky, they could make a 10% gain of $2,000. If that same $20,000 were put down on a house and $80,000 were financed and the house only increases in value by 5%, that person has made $5,000. That is a 25% return on the $20,000 that they personally invested.

Real estate uses other people's money, so the return is based on a much larger amount of money than what a person invests. That is why the stock market's ability to make a higher return is immaterial. Also, the real estate market is much less volatile than the stock market is. Play your cards right and your property can continue to create positive cash flow during the worst of times.

Chapter 7: Various Lead Generation Methods

While it is generally easier to find people who want to sell some property, it is harder to locate the motivated sellers among them who are willing to unload their properties at bargain prices.

If you are a wholesaler of property, you have to get property at your pre-determined bargain price or else there is no room for both you and the buyer/investor to make money. That means you need to target motivated sellers of property when you advertise your services for the purpose of generating good leads.

Just as there are cheap and more expensive types of investments that you can invest in, there are cheap and more expensive ways to generate leads.

Top Ways to Find Motivated Sellers

1. **Put Out Bandit Signs**

   Bandit signs are inexpensive ones with metal frames that you stick into the ground close to roads. They generally say something like, "We buy houses fast," or "Need cash?"

   They have your contact phone number, which is a Google Voice number or something like that which is not your personal phone number. They also contain your website that has a squeeze page that forces them to send you their contact information.

People see your signs and they then call you, leave their call-back number or else they send you their contact information electronically and you call them back. You call them back and ascertain whether or not they are a motivated seller or could become one. If they are not motivated enough to cut a good deal, you need to walk away.

People have a couple of seconds to see your sign, so put several of them within a span of two miles. Put them on vacant land, on busy streets in the high-grass yards of vacant houses that are not owned by a bank. Try to find the slow-moving traffic streets, but don't put them on street corners or you will be fined.

2. Code Violators

The code violators are people who were fined for not cutting their grass or keeping too many vehicles in the front yard, etc., and they typically cannot afford to pay the fine. They fast become desperate to sell the property so that they can pay the fine and stay out of jail.

You will have to go to the courthouse to find out who those people are. While there during your first visit, you will likely have to quote the Freedom of Information Act to get them to let you see the list because they will likely refuse to give you the list of code breakers.

After they agree to let you see it, they will likely tell you to give them some time. You come back the next day with a dollar for their trouble and get the list. Do this every two weeks (minus the freedom of information act part) for more leads. Law enforcement people will help you too if you tell them what you do because you would be helping them to get properties up to code.

You call the code violators on the phone and ask them if they know of anybody who wants to sell their property, but you don't tell them you know they are a code violator.

3. Evictions

You see the sheriff there and people taking belongings out of the house. You approach the owner and determine whether they are the home owner and, if they are, whether or not they are desperate enough to sell the house immediately and at a bargain price.

4. Burned-Out Landlords, from "For Rent" Signs

You notice a property that has a "For Rent" sign out front, and you notice that it remains unrented for months. What you can do is to write the landlord's number down that you see on the sign and call him on the phone to see whether he would like to sell his rental property. Try to tactfully find out why he can't rent it and other details about his situation. The landlord may be just tired of being a landlord, or he may not have enough money to repair the house. Find out whether the landlord is ready to get rid of their problem house and make a little money in the process.

5. Burned-Out Landlords, from Court

You can find burned-out landlords are by hanging around the courthouse. Landlords who lose cases in court that have to do with a tenant may need to come up with a lot of money quickly so they can pay the tenant what the court orders them to pay or else they will go to jail. Their situation may persuade them to get out of the rental business. It becomes obvious to them that they could get rid of all of their troubles if they could quickly sell their run-down property. Those are burned-out landlords who are highly motivated to quickly sell their rental home, even at a bargain price.

6. Internet Marketing

You can try to advertise your service to "buy houses" on Craigslist, but the site is saturated these days with ads from wholesalers.

7. Search Craigslist

Look for "Must sell" advertisements on Craigslist. Call them on the phone to see how motivated they really are and how cheaply they would sell their property.

8. Use Bird Dogs

Advertise on Craigslist in the "Etc" category that you are looking for people to scout out property for them. Advertise that you will pay $500.00 for every house that they locate for you that you buy. When they call you, explain to them what you do, what you expect from them, and that your attorney cuts the checks out to your bird dogs at the closings of properties that the bird dogs locate for you.

You need to manage these people if they are new to this gig because many of them will waste your time by calling you a lot or giving you leads for properties that end up being listed in realtor MLS listings.

9. Social Networking

Facebook, Twitter and Linkedin are warm contacts (hopefully) that you

Will have already established rapport with. You type, "I want to buy a

house in (location). If you know of anybody wanting to sell their house, let

me know and I will pay you $500.00." Also stipulate that you are not

looking for MLS listings.

10. Post Cards

Send yellow post cards out to only the people who have a lot of equity in the property you wish to buy.

Understand that the low-margin neighborhoods have less competition. If you are just getting started in the business, it is advisable that you get your experience, make your mistakes, and build your confidence in the smaller paying properties.

Secondly, post cards are a numbers game. The response rate for most direct mailers, such as post cards, across various industries is about 1%. However, in the property wholesaling business, the response rate is better than 2%. If you send out 2,500 advertisement post cards, you can expect to generat 50 leads (2,500 x 0.02).

Only one person out of every five leads actually sounds motivated enough to sell their property at a bargain price. That means that you make an offer to only 10 of the 50 leads that you got from the post cards. The other people wanted too much money for their property or else they don't want to make a deal right now.

Only one in three of those 10 people sign on the dotted line, so you have three of the 10 motivated sellers under contract. Once you have sellers under contract, you find buyers for the properties, reassign your contracts to them, and make $5,000 between the three of them at closing.

The batch of 2,500 cards cost you $1,250 to mail out and you got back $5,000. You quadrupled your money on the low end of the market! Mailing out 2,500 cards will still cost you $1,250 to mail out when you move into the higher end of the spectrum, so your return on your investment only gets better.

11. Expired Listings

Ask a real estate agent to let you see their expired real estate listings.

Maybe a fee per peek.

12. Advertising Pens

Give various U-Haul/storage facilities and gas stations bundles of your advertising pens to give out. Many of the people who frequent those kinds of places have just moved out a house that they need to unload.

13. Automated Emailer

When you have a website set up, people can see it advertised on your bandit signs, Craigslist, etc. When people visit your website, they put their contact information on the form you have on your website. It would be helpful to have your website set up to email you that contact information whenever somebody fills out the form on your website.

14. Door Knocking

This method is not comfortable for a lot of people, but it is an effective, cheap and low-tech way to generate leads. All you do is ask people for information they might have about somebody possibly needing to sell property in a hurry.

Online Research to Locate Profitable Neighborhoods

Bandit signs and post cards target everybody, but advertising to just the people who would be most interested in selling their properties would make better use of your time, effort and marketing dollars. Consider targeting property owners who live out of state.

An out-of-state owner may have just inherited property from a parent or from some other family member. Maybe an employer gave the owner transfer orders and the owner had to leave their home behind in a hurry.

Whatever the reason a property owner lives in some state other than where their property is, the property is often considered by their owner as being too far away to effectively manage a renter or to assure that the grass is mowed and that the home is well maintained. These property owners are highly likely to view the far-flung properties as burdens they would almost pay someone to take off of their hands!

There are a few online sites that an investor can use to find neighborhoods that have a high number of homes that have out-of-state owners. One site you can use to find these people is **www.listsource.com**. You must go through particular steps to find these out-of-state home owners, however. The steps are as follows:

1. Decide on the larger cities that you wouldn't mind wholesaling in. You may be driving to these cities quite a bit.

2. Find the zip codes within those cities that contain the highest populations.

   a. Find all zip codes within your desired city (do one city at a time) by doing a Google (or Yahoo, etc.) search using the words, "zip codes" followed by the city and state you are researching.

   b. For instance, you would find the zip codes for Dallas by typing "zip codes Dallas, Texas" in the search box.Look to see which zip codes have the very highest populations in them, and write those zip codes down.

3. Build a list on **www.listsource.com**.   You will complete several steps for each zip code as you go.

   a. Get onto the listsource.com website.

   b. Click on the "Build List" tab.

      1.) Geography – Type in one of your highly populated zip codes. Click on "Add." This tells you how many properties are in that zip code.

   c. Click on the "Property" tab.

      1.) Click on "Last market sale date," "Last 6 months," and "Add." This tells you how many homes sold within the last 6 months.

d. Click on the "Options" tab.

    1.) Click on "Absentee control." Click "No preference" on corporate owned. Leave everything else alone. What comes up is how many houses were likely bought as investments.

e. Click on the "Property" tab again.

    1.) Click on "Property Type" if you want to specialize.

        a.) Click on "...SFR" for single family residence, for example. Then click on "Add."

f. Click on the "Property" tab yet again.

    1.) Click on "Last Market Sales Price."

    2.) Click on the range(s) that represent the bottom half in that zip code:

        a.) Click on "One to $50,000" and "$50,000 to $100,000." Nineteen is considered a lot.

4. Repeat the process for every zip code you listed, using only the last screen and do the following:

a. Highlight the zip code that was added and hit "Remove."

b. Replace it with the next zip code of interest. Parameters remain.
c. Cross off areas where few investment deals are made.
d. Notate the zip codes with the highest number of investments.

Marketing Trends

*Traditional marketing - M*arketing in general is changing and becoming more targeted and effective. If you were a real estate agent (not a wholesaler) trying to generate leads in the traditional way, you would throw a lot of money into advertising that focuses on the product rather than on the customer, and you would get a small return on your investment.

You basically would get your name out there enough that people start to call you. If you hold an open house, you have lots of lonely hours coupled with a few awkward moments where people nervously glance your way, you exchange a few cordial remarks, and then you ask them straight up to sign in, handing over their contact information when they don't know you. A lot of wasted money and time is spent doing business this way.

New marketing trend - What smart agents are doing these days is to focus on the needs of customers rather than throwing out property/product information. Agents find out what customers want and who the customers are.

Customers want the agent's knowledge and support. They want to know what's in it for them to do business with that agent. What would set that agent apart from all the rest?

One way the smart agent would generate leads while accomplishing all of this is to hold a question and answer session that is on the topic of a customer's first home. The public gets answers to questions and they get to know the agent a little bit. Some of them then feel comfortable enough to give the agent their email address.

The agent then follows up with an email campaign that gives the people additional tips to consider, etc. They are valuable emails to those people. For the agent, the agent's name is being kept in front of those people and rapport is being established. Rather than being just a pestering salesman, the agent is viewed as a helpful resource and the person they will select when they are ready to buy their first home.

Apply the new marketing trends to your wholesaling business - It is not much different when you are lead generating as an investment property buyer. One thing that newbie quick flippers/wholesalers often fail to do is to spend time getting to know prospects before putting any sort of pressure on them. You may call them five times before you get down to business.

You need motivated sellers. Not only are they the ones who will let you have the property for the bargain price you need it at, but you are solving some problem they have. You need to find out what their problem/motivation is and target that need, becoming a problem solver in their eyes.

Conclusion

Thank you again for purchasing this book. I hope it was informative and able to provide you with all of the tools you need to achieve your investment goals.

You've learned what the mindset is that wealthy people have. You learned about the four ways that people invest in real estate and what the pitfalls of each strategy are. You know which one (s) of those four types of investing would work for your financial situation and for your knowledge, skills and abilities.

You now have a knowledge of the many ways that you can locate distressed properties and their owners. Your knowledge of property scouting and price negotiation will help you to do any of the investment strategies.

You have some sample forms that you may need for hiring rehab work to be done. You also know more about the marketing aspect of the business.

The next step is to do the mental exercises mentioned. Then you need to get yourself organized and create your marketing tools. If you plan to do wholesaling, look into the legality of it in your state. You will also benefit from a mentor who knows the ropes of wholesaling if that is the strategy you intend to do.

Finally, if you found this book useful in any way, a good review on Amazon is always appreciated!

Description

You can take control of your financial future through strategic real estate investing. Yes, you can. You absolutely can, so don't let anybody tell you differently.

The value of the dollar continues to dwindle as the cost of living continues to rise. Meanwhile, full-time jobs get harder to find and to keep long-term. People are often either unemployed or underemployed. People no longer have money saved up. The future looks scary.

The middle class has all but disappeared, creating a society of the haves and the have-nots. The have-nots are now looking for long-term effective solutions to their ongoing financial worries. Since the source of these wide-spread problems comes from other people in one way or another, smart people realize that they need to do some sort of self-employment and/or smart investing.

Real estate has long been something that people have not only made decent money with, but have made absolute fortunes with. Some people go into real estate as licensed agents, and a few of those agents go on to be brokers. Other people invest in real estate, and real estate investment for the beginner is the topic of this book.

Everyone knows that a person who has several thousand dollars can buy rental homes and make money that way. Those of us who don't have thousands of dollars tend to just give up on the notion of making big money through real estate.

What is not commonly known, however, are the different ways that a person could get into real estate investing with little money and work their way up into the easier, more profitable types of real estate investing. Therefore, while it is a have and have-not society, there are ways a person can bridge the gap and get to the other side through smart real estate investment strategies.

This book explains the four broad categories of real estate investment and many of the sub-categories. Two of the four broad categories do not require a person to have a lot of money going into them, and two of them do. This book directs the reader to the various ways to make money that are available to people from all walks of life. It also details the pitfalls that can come with doing some of these strategies if a person is not careful.

The mindset of millionaires is discussed, as are the many ways that real estate investors can locate motivated sellers who are out there, just waiting for somebody to take their real estate problems off of their hands.

Imagine yourself in the future going from having few dates to attracting many admirers. If you are married, imagine yourself being able to hold your head high when your family looks at you instead of wondering why you can't manage to do a better job of providing for them. Imagine yourself surrounded with more positive circles of friends.

Dream bigger and you can imagine yourself going from rags to absolute riches. Donald Trump started with one million dollars, made some mistakes, learned from his mistakes and went on to build an absolute empire over the years in real estate.

Most of us, though, would have to start off with less than a thousand dollars to put into any real estate venture. Take heart because there are ways to start small and end up making big money. Let this little book get you off to an informed start.

www.ingramcontent.com/pod-product-compliance
Lightning Source LLC
Chambersburg PA
CBHW051246170526
45165CB00004B/1595